Soul: Echoes of Self

Trinity Allen

BookLeaf Publishing

India | USA | UK

Presentation by *BookLeaf Publishing*

Web: www.bookleafpub.com

E-mail: info@bookleafpub.com

ISBN: 9789363308954

First edition 2024

*To Mommy and Moon, whose love shines
through shadows and lights my path forward.*

ACKNOWLEDGEMENT

First and foremost, I want to thank my beautiful mother, who has always given me the space to see myself and explore my passions. Your unwavering support and love have been my foundation.

To my grandmother, thank you for keeping me sane and always listening to everything I have to say. Your wisdom and patience have been my anchor.

To all of my friends, thank you for supporting me and always believing in me. Your encouragement has fueled my journey and kept me moving forward.

To my moon, thank you for always loving me and speaking light into my journey. Your presence has been a beacon of hope and strength.

I also want to thank myself for taking the leap and trusting my intuition. This book would not exist without that inner courage.

Last, but most importantly, I thank God for loving and protecting me throughout my entire life. Your divine guidance has led me to this moment, and I am forever grateful.

PREFACE

Soul: Abstract Echoes of Self is my first poetry collection, a dream I've finally brought to life. This book is more than just a collection of poems—it's a window into the parts of my soul that I keep to myself. Each piece here carries a fragment of my journey, from moments of deep self-discovery to the raw emotions of love and everything in between.

Writing poetry has always been my way of making sense of the world. It's been my confidant through highs and lows, and now, I'm ready to share these intimate pieces with you. These poems are deeply personal and vulnerable, revealing in a way that scares me more deeply than most of you will ever know.

As you read through these pages, you'll journey with me into the complexities of identity, love, and the introspective thoughts that shape us. I hope these poems resonate with you, offering a sense of connection and understanding.

Thank you for joining me on this path. I hope *Soul* speaks to you as it has to me.

You:Me

Somatically spiritual...
I hear you in my thoughts,
The voice in my head,
Sitting in between brain rot.
Ultimately, lovers born in hurt.
Sound waves to shock waves,
Humans born to lurk.
To each what they cannot understand:
Lifeless,
Unborn,
Like a child to the womb.
A sponge,
Kisses to foreheads,
Healed interlopers.
A life before me,
Me before you.

Forgotten Self

Interference-

A path interrupted.

Knowledge beyond that which is given.
A mind taken.

Losing parts of you,
Disappeared memories.
No first kiss,
No first child.

That which makes you,
Beyond time,
Yet lost to it.

You question who you are,
Reminders everywhere,
From everyone...

Disappointment when it fades back in.
A fractured thought,
Distant from your beloved,
Pitied by your children.

This full, beautiful experience:
Revolutions,
Riots,
Minds met,
Lives changed.

An invisible lifetime,
That even you have left forgotten.

Psyche's Reverie

Alchemical girl,
I wonder if we're all born in a mortuary,
Where we'll find our deaths,
If there's ever truly rest.

Singing soliloquies
From far-removed realities,
The rarity of that which can truly understand me.
Watching leaves as they fall to dust,
Fixing engines as they fall to rust.
A new and fragile trust,

Continuances of sadness and songbirds,
Righteousness and wrong words.
Internalizing the spiritual,
Externalizing the fearful,
In preparation for an earful.

All these screaming doves flying past—
I can feel it coming up in my throat,
The urge to scream alongside,
The urge to just delete what I wrote.

Running from Myself?

There are some days when I'm scared of
knowing myself,
I'm scared of reason...
understanding the dichotomy between me and
my demons,
Scared of who I'd become if I stopped
people-pleasing...

In some ways, that's easy:
Stop asking questions and just be me.
I know most days my pain stunts my growth.
My path feels like a tightrope,
I'm walking on air,
Forgetting which step is the right one.

Understand that I might run
From all these things that make me feel all these
things,
On the edge of this cliff,
Standing far too close to the brink.

Silence After...

And after darkness

There is this blissful silence

Tears shed into my pillow

Wondering why I feel like this

Why I can't sleep alone

And my eyes are never really dry

Up for days on end

Pretty and sleep deprived

No one really likes me when I'm sad

There's less of me to entertain

Less of me to give

Hemorrhaging air like a poked lung

Don't I remind you of rotted fruit

So sweet and soft

Until you realize all the damage time has
done….

Sunkissed

Gifts given
Love felt
A loss between our beautiful parts
Like puzzle pieces—
Fitted to one and other
moonlight in colorful sky
opposite yet same
Intertwined?
Live-wires in the same socket
I can feel your current
Will you shock me?
Sunkissed skin
free and restless
Just us, and what we've been
Fall in love with the summer again?

Surface Love

Entranced,
Watching you, watching me,
Seeing all the things I wish you could be.
Almost an obsession,
A tightrope between
Me, you, and this pedestal.
My manic pixie dream girl.
Why question what you think?
I'm preferential
To dreaming about your potential.
I love who you can be.
Infatuation with you passes,
Saturation in these rose-colored glasses.
I love the way you look at me,
As long as it's not too deeply.
Don't peek too close, or else you truly see me.
Something in me loves the surface of us,
These perfect masks we put on for each other,
Actresses feigning real trust.
The people we make each other out to be,
More than what we are,
Less than what we could be.

Golden Butterfly's Lament

Coasting away,
Like rotting fruit on sunny days.
I wonder if God hears me when I pray,
If I'd ever be the person asked to stay.
Something like a golden butterfly,
Beautiful and fragile,
Sight unseen,
A rare occurrence.
Too much and not enough,
A weak ocean current,
The kind that only pulls you and forgets the rest,
Drowning only your lungs.
Maybe there I can finally get rest.
I see the world and all its tears;
I can't help but cry.
I see children and all their fears;
I can't help but lie.
Tell them all is well and always will be,
Hiding the realness of tragedy.
I look around and see people
And their painted pictures and painted histories.
I can't see your souls,
So who are you really?
Are you a golden butterfly too?

Jumping In

A heart so big it opens doors without trying.
Pretty girl with a pretty heart—
Not something you're used to finding.
But that's all they see.
If only you knew how much I laugh to keep
from crying—
How much I use my love to cope
And keep from feeling alone.
How hard it is to show the real me
So I shove my soul into a poem.
My capacity to love is all I got,
So I jump in feet first—not knowing where I'll
land or in what spot.
With a chest like a wound
Open to everyone
But easily hurt.
I've seen the darkest corners of the world—
Walked out with my chin up,
Wearing my pain as a shroud,
Holding tight to the parts of me that I refuse to
freely give.
Giving grace,
Knowing I can make me proud.
In moments of fear, I promised myself
I would always do the things I wasn't allowed.

Never afraid to show my scars or give my love.
To me, that's what being alive is about.

My Moon

Can you understand how I love you?
I love you unconditionally.
I love you irrevocably.
I love you undoubtedly.
I love you like you're the moon to my stars.
I love you because it's an honor to be in the
presence of someone
whose heartbeat I can feel across a room
I love you in a way that makes me remember
there is true joy in trust.
I love you openly,
Wholeheartedly.
I get why people are scared by the depths of real
love.
It's infinite.
It holds through storms
And bends with hurt.
That solid type of love,
The kind that never leaves,
Only stretches with distance and difference.
And with all this love,
I love you.

Mirror—

A mirror
We stand
Face to face
Me watching you...
Watch me
Eyes sink to the ground-
Guilty shadows
False promises
Shatter me.
Love me?
Separate yet same
Pain interrupted
Shared through us
Feel what I feel.
Damage inflicted
Heart to heart,
Soul tied
Similarity
How can you see me
Without seeing yourself.

Sweet Girl

And so I break off sections of the most
 delectable, most selectable, candy-coated
sexiest parts of me.
I put them on a platter.
Am I sweet enough for you?
Does my sex appeal
Make you forget
Your sex doesn't appeal to me?
Eyes shining like the sadness in the stars.
Do you think I like the way you hurt me?
The things you took from me I'll never even
know.
Too young to even remember the shadow
Of how I would've grown
If only my safety hadn't been stolen from me
By someone, I should have never even known.
Life's cycles have shown me that you were
never meant to be the only,
Just the first one who couldn't keep his boy parts
to himself.

Trustfalls

A scarred heart is all I can put to use.
This kind of love doesn't put you on a pedestal
Or make you an ideal.
It just is—
Utterly unconditional,
Sometimes painful,
Based upon the person you are alone.
The beauty I see inside your heart,
An ocean current.
The way my chest caves when you smile at me,
Something like a hurricane.
Looking at the stars,
Remembering how stunning you are underneath,
Knowing you're worth every poem,
Every tear.
Can I show you the parts of me no one's seen?
Would you judge me?
Heavy and passionate,
Impulsive and a little unhinged.
Could you love me anyway?
I know it's fast,
But we were born to love and be loved,
The both of us.
So I'm risking my heart and falling
uncontrollably.
Catch me?

Her.

All these shadows in the corners of my room,
Me questioning all the ways that I love you.
You call me, and say you miss me,
And now you say you love me.

I can't help but see her.
wonder if you miss her,
If I fill that hole for you,
If I'm everything she used to be.

I wonder if that kind of love was it for you—
Soulmates in tandem,
A pair of two.
You had to leave her,
So now I'm wondering if you love me
In all the ways you used to need her.
Sometimes when I look in your eyes,
I see longing for what could've been.

You want it all for us;
At least that's what you say.
You want home with me.
Is it the kind where
Her shadow sometimes lurks in the hallways?

Rest Stop

What are we?
Do you wonder? Do you care?
Or has your respect for me in the face of my
love for you
seen your opinion of me go so low
there's nothing to think about?
Your offer to be friends simply a way
for you to spectate my pain
and my presumed lack of self-respect?
To watch me adore you
while giving nothing of yourself,
Not a friend and definitely never a lover.
Do I seem angry?
A true cry for you to stay,
To open up,
To pour into me the way I have you.
No matter how you choose to define us,
Otherwise, you just become a holdout from a life
I don't want anymore—
An energy
I won't hold anymore.
Sometimes I wish you would come home,
But I'm realizing now I was never a home for
you,
Just a rest stop on the way to a destination
I can't see.

Unknown ID

I heard you lost someone
I felt a twinge in my fingers
Urging me to call…
I haven't felt that in—
I think of the ways you held me up,
The ways you broke me down
Teaching me what love isn't
How being gentle is a kindness not given freely.
I think we always cherish that first childhood
love
The one that breaks you the most
Those thoughts about how it felt to fall
no expectations
Or far too many
In the end, only to become strangers
Subject to stray thoughts
And stray poems
I never did pick up my phone.

Tunnel Vision

In this word I tell you that I see you.
I see you for the things you think me blind to.
I see you for the words unsaid,
Those parts of your soul gone unseen.
I see the love that has grown arms with which to
carry me.
I see the heartache still healing,
Like a bullet that ricocheted and left its mark.
I see all this knowledge of life
And yet still just a human learning where to
start.
I see a protector.
I see a back that would hide me from the world
if I asked.
I see your courageous spirit
And shoulders that hold more than they should.
When I look in your eyes, I see a new softness,
A light that I would feed endlessly if I could,
A confidence in a version of yourself even you
have never seen before.
I see the emotions you fearlessly bear.
So when I stare,
When I look too long, it's noticeable.
Know I'm not looking at the vessel you were
blessed with;

My eyes and my heart see deeper,
Entranced by rare energy,
The kind that's true—
seeing you.

Evangeline

Falling in love with my peculiarities…
Like the stain glass windows
on the wings of a firefly
My parts each their own
transient beauty
Following my path
Causing hurricanes on the other side of the
world
To accept what is
understand my path moves worlds away
Intimate with the impact
quite like lovers
Who am I?

Inner Child Work

Acceptance of my past I'm still finding.
Wipe away moonlit tears when you're crying.
That little girl inside me—
You,
A root underneath my tree.
Soft flesh still molding,
Breathtaking in your naivety.
I will hold you in my arms,
Kiss you on your head,
Tell you everything will be okay,
And tuck you into bed.
I am your home,
Your rock.
I give to you my imagination,
The kind of giving that never stops.
I watch over you as you dance through fields.
The tiniest version of myself
Will know life.

My Shadow and Me.

Can you see
That there are two of me?
Dual personalities,
Separate entities.

A shadow self who
Finds past me's to embody,
A surface self who
Holds no mastery over feeling lonely.
A third eye unseen,
A choice to be all the lost versions,
Be again all the people I haven't been.

Searching for the dead,
Digging graves for the known.
Duality,
A wing balancing,
Integrating.

So much love blooms—
Me and you,
Shadow.
I am seen in the darkness.

Trinity

Waiting for darkness to outlive me
Arriving on the end of oblivious thought,
Cycles arriving in triangles
A Trinity
truth through my namesake
A life beyond what I was given…
A path I carve with my name in each obstacle
Reminders that growth never comes with ease
True love only seen when courage outlasts fear
And the questions of life fall out of favor….
Instead only finding answers where hardships lie
Peace
Creation from the ashes of broken matter
Building new versions of me
A labor of love.